Becoming A
Woman of Beauty

by Patricia L. Welch

Becoming A Woman of Beauty

2013

Welch Publishing ISBN:978-0-578-13407-9

Printed in the United States of America

Table of Contents

Acknowledgements

Besides thanking God, I want to thank the following people for their invaluable help as I studied, taught, and now publish this book on Becoming A Woman of Beauty.

Professor Chris Miller of Word of Life Bible Institute and Cedarville College, who helped edit my original manuscript and gave me wonderful encouragement. Thank you, Chris.

The teenage girls in my Sunday school class in upstate NY who heard these lessons first.

The ladies in "Women of Grace" life group who listen to me teach each week and give me valuable feedback and encouragement as I witness spiritual growth in their lives.

And last but not least, a big thank you to my husband, Francis Welch, who faithfully reads over my work, chapter by chapter, makes helpful suggestions, and challenges me to be creative by his insightful questions and comments. ♥

How To Gain The Most From This Study

In this generation, busyness and stress abound. Now more than ever, you need to slow down enough to focus on God and His Word. If necessary, plan to start your day earlier in order to get back to the basics of your Christian faith.

Choose a time that is convenient for you and not when you know you will be interrupted. Find a special place to concentrate on God and what He is going to reveal to you Make Psalm 119:18 the daily prayer of your time with God. "Open my eyes, Lord, that I may see wondrous things in your Law." Stick with it and treat it as an important appointment with God, and keep that appointment no matter what.

Whether you spend 15 minutes or an hour or more each day in the Word of God, ask Him to fill you with His Holy Spirit and to give you wisdom and understanding as you go through this study.

- ♥ Purpose to take the time to read and think through each chapter carefully, and not rush through trying to answer the questions.

- ♥ Writing out Bible verses is never a waste of time, so take the time to do this. The Word of God is powerful.

- ♥ After you have completed a lesson, take the time to read back over both the lesson and your answers, and ask God to impress upon your heart what He wants you to remember and apply to your life. You might want to keep a notebook of these things.

- ♥ Practice "immediate obedience" to anything God tells you to do.

- ♥ Take time to talk to God in prayer after each lesson and thank Him for any insights and wisdom He has given you.

Introduction

The main focus of women, more than ever before, is to be beautiful and sexy. Women join fitness clubs, spend time in tanning salons, and make weekly or monthly appointments for manicures, pedicures and massages. They spend money on botox and surgeries that promise to make them look at least 10-20 years younger.

Women are jogging, playing tennis, exercising and dieting in various ways to keep their bodies in shape. They are also buying millions of dollars worth of makeup, hair products, clothes and jewelry, all to make themselves more beautiful.

There is nothing wrong with wanting to look beautiful - I think we're wired that way. However, we are starting these improvements on the outside, when we should be starting on the inside and working outward. Even a woman without natural physical beauty can be thought of as beautiful if she develops her inner qualities and uses them for the Lord.

The title of this study is "Becoming A Woman of Beauty," and is based on Romans 12:1,2:

> "I beseech you, therefore, brethren, by the mercies of God, that you present your bodies a living sacrifice, holy, acceptable unto God, which is your reasonable service. And be not conformed to this world, but be transformed by the renewing of your mind, that you may prove what is that good, and acceptable, and perfect will of God."

We will learn what these verses mean and how to make them practical in your life. I trust this study will help you to determine God's will for your life in the area of true beauty. To start us off on our journey, I would like to share with you a poem God gave me when I was putting this study together.

My Body . . . A Living Sacrifice ©

Romans 12:1-2
by Patricia L. Welch

© Beverley Lu Latter

Here are my hands, Lord . . .

Use them for your glory. Help me to reach out to others and to make a difference in their lives. Help me to soothe and to comfort, and to serve, never touching unclean things . . . the things you don't want me to have.

Here are my feet, Lord . . .

Guide them. Direct them. Keep them on the right path. Help me not to stumble and trip. Help me not to wander and get lost by following Satan's detours. Help my feet to stay on that right path and to walk in the Light of your Word.

Here is my mouth, Lord . . .

Help me to be kind and loving, building others up with my words, not tearing down. Help me to tell others about you. Help me not to taste that which is evil, but to partake only of those things that you want me to have.

Here are my eyes, Lord . . .

> Help them to be focused only on you, and not on the false picture of sin that Satan paints. Let me not ever think that sin is beautiful, but something that sent you to the cross to suffer, and bleed and die for me!

Here are my ears, Lord . . .

> Help me to always listen to your Word and obey it, because it is the only source of truth. Help me not to listen to Satan's voice, for he is a liar and never tells the truth. Help me to know the voice of my Shepherd, and let me not follow any other.

Here is my mind, Lord . . .

> Fill it with Thy Word that I might be transformed into the person you want me to be. Help me to study, and as I do, give me wisdom and understanding. Help me to glean principles and insight from your Word to apply to my own life and to help others also.

Here is my heart, Lord . . .

> Help it always to be tender and sensitive to you. Keep it from being hardened and uncaring. Help it not to be dirtied by impure thoughts, which in turn, lead to impure acts. "Create in me a clean heart, O God, and renew a right spirit within me."

Chapter 1

Your Eyes

Looking at sin as it really is – Dirty, ugly and degrading

In this lesson we are going to think about our eyes in relationship to being beautiful. Beautiful eyes stay focused on God and His will for our lives. Sometimes we are tempted to look away from God when our enemy, Satan, promises exciting results of sin. In case you haven't found out yet, Satan is a liar! In fact the Bible describes him as the "father of lies" (John 8:44).

There are some Bible people who disobeyed God because something God prohibited looked good to them. They forgot that God loved them and would provide for all their needs.

Satan presented something to each of these people that on the outside looked glamorous and exciting, but after they had sinned, each person found out that sin took them further than they wanted to go, kept them longer than they wanted to stay, cost them more than they wanted to pay, and caused them more guilt, grief and heartache than they ever imagined.

Eve

What was God's commandment to Adam and Eve in Genesis 2:16-17?_____

_____

_____

How did Satan make sin sound exciting to Eve in Genesis 3:5_____

_____

_____

Why did Eve obey Satan instead of God? (Genesis 3:6)

_____

_____

_____

What didn't Eve realize about Satan's feelings for her?
(I Peter 5:8)_____

_____

What were the consequences Adam & Eve had to deal with
because of disobedience? (Genesis 3:8,16,23-24; 4:1-8)

_____

_____

_____

_____

What far-reaching effect did their disobedience have?
(Romans 5:12)

_____

_____

In what ways did Satan lie to Eve? (Genesis 3:4-5)

_____

_____

_____

Potiphar's Wife

How did Potiphar's wife use her eyes in an ungodly and
foolish way? (Genesis 39:6-7)

_____

_____

What commandment of God did she break? (Exodus 20:14)

_____

How did Joseph react and why? (Genesis 39:8-9)

_____

_____

_____

Do you think Potiphar's wife repented? (Genesis 39:10-20)
Explain your answer._____

_____

_____

What could she have done? (II Timothy 2:22)

_____

_____

Lot's Wife

How did the Lord feel about the city in which Lot and his
wife lived? (Genesis 18:20)

_____

What did God decide to do about it? (Genesis 19:13)

_____

What was the reason Lot and his family were saved out of
the city? (Genesis 19:16)

_____

How did Lot's wife use her eyes in a foolish way and what
happened to her? (Genesis 19:26)

_____

_____

What specific commandment of God did Lot's wife break?
(Genesis 19:17)

_____

11

Do you ever look back with longing at the sin that God has saved you from? Why or why not?

_____

_____

_____

_____

_____

King David

What did David's eyes linger on? (II Samuel 11:2)

_____

What did David do? (II Samuel 11:3-4)

_____

_____

_____

What was the immediate consequence of his sin?
(II Samuel 11:5)

_____

What other sin did adultery lead to? (II Samuel 11:14-15)

_____

What was one of the consequences that David had to pay for his sin and why? (II Samuel 12:14)

_____

_____

_____

Other consequences of sin included David's daughter Tamar being raped by one of her brothers. David's son Absalom killed his brother Ammon and also tried to kill David. And then Absalom himself was killed.

What promise of God explains the consequences that came to David? (Galatians 6:7-8)

_____

_____

_____

_____

Making it personal . . .

Eve was tempted to eat of the tree that God had forbidden so that she could be wise like God. The end result of her sin was loss of fellowship with God, loss of her home in Eden, pain during childbirth, a son who killed his brother, and all of mankind down through the ages falling under the curse of sin and death.

Potiphar's wife was tempted by an anticipated sexual experience with a good looking man who her husband respected. The end result of her sin was rejection, humiliation, and a lasting testimony of her foolishness for all to read.

Lot's wife was tempted to look back at the evil God had saved her from instead of keeping her focus on God. The end result of her sin was that she was turned into a pillar of salt.

David's temptation was a beautiful woman who was someone else's wife. The end result of his sin was that he got the woman, but also received heartbreak and sorrow beyond his imagination.

What about you? How are you tempted when Satan comes to entice you? Do you look upon and let your eyes linger on what he promises, or do you trust and obey God?

There is a price to pay for using our eyes in the wrong way. We cannot escape the consequences of sin no matter how beautiful a picture Satan paints for us.

<u>Making it prayerful</u> . . .

Dear Lord, I pray the Holy Spirit will convict me of sin when I use my eyes in a wrong way and that I will have a spirit of repentance. Help me to keep my eyes focused on you and never on the false picture of sin that Satan paints. Help me to realize that the enemy desires my destruction.
Thank you Lord, for your protection.

Chapter 2

Your Eyes
Looking Towards God Who Provides
Victory Over Sin

In this continuing lesson on eyes, we're going to focus on and try to catch a vision of God. Without a vision of God, our eyes will be looking at the false picture of sin that Satan paints, and this will lead to sin, and ultimately spiritual death.

"Where there is no vision, the people perish"
Proverbs 29:18

We get a vision of God in the following ways: Through His handiwork, through visions of old, through studying His attributes.

A vision of God through His handiwork

God is the Creator of everything. Think of things God has created and what each one tells you about God.

Mountains –
Ocean –
Flowers or snowflakes –
Baby –
Sunset -
Kitten or puppy -
What are a few other things that impress you about God's creation and why?

Overall, God is highly creative, intricate and wise. He is the author of all beauty.

God creates everything for a purpose. God has a purpose for your life and mine, and we need to ask Him to guide our lives so that we will fulfill that purpose. As the created, we should never turn to our Creator and say that we know better than He does what we were created for, and try to do things our way. God loves us and knows what is best for us and how to give us the most fulfillment and joy.

A vision of God through visions of old

God used to make Himself known to people through visions. We can learn more about God by studying these visions. Look up the following Scripture passages in the Bible and write down everything you see about God in each vision:

Isaiah's Vision - Isaiah 6:1-5

Isaiah was a great prophet of God, but what was his reaction when He saw God in this vision? Isaiah 6:5

Ezekiel's Vision - Ezekiel 43:1-2

Ezekiel was also a great prophet of God, but what was his reaction to this vision? Ezekiel 43:3

Daniel's Vision - Daniel 10:5-6

What was Daniel's reaction when he saw this vision of God? Daniel 10:8-9

What was John's reaction after seeing this vision?
Revelation 22:8

How do you think Isaiah, Ezekiel, Daniel and John felt after
seeing visions like these?_____
_____
_____
_____

God is so much more than our human minds can
comprehend. We need to humbly bow ourselves before
God and worship Him, realizing how small and unworthy we
are, and how big our God is!

A vision of God through studying His attributes

God no longer comes to us in visions, but He has given us His Holy Word, the Bible, so that we can study and learn more about Him.

Match the following attributes of God with their definitions (a dictionary will help):

Immutable   **Righteous**   **Omnipotent**
Omniscient   **Sovereign**   **Truth**
Eternal   **Omnipresent**   **Just**   **Love**

_____ - He is in control (Psalm 47:2). There is no-one higher to go to. He's the King above all the earth.

_____ - He is perfect, holy (Deut. 32:4). God hates sin and I need to be cleansed daily from my sin. I need to realize in my heart that it was my sin that nailed Jesus to the cross.

_____ - Always does the right thing (I John 1:9). He keeps His promises. He will never go against His Word. He forgives my sins because of Jesus. Chastens when necessary when I try to hang on to my sin.

_____ - Always does what is best (I Cor. 13). I can feel secure because He'll always bring me good and not evil. Nothing can ever separate me from His love. No man can pluck me out of the Father's hand – He loves me that much - He'll never let me go.

_____ - Without beginning or end (Jer. 10:10). He is everlasting. This is awesome and makes me worship. If we had a God we could totally understand, He wouldn't be God.

_____ - He knows everything (Proverbs 5:21). He knows the end from the beginning. He has all the answers. Nothing ever takes Him by surprise. I need to go to Him for wisdom.

_____ - Everything is within His view (Prov.15:3) There is nothing His eyes do not see. We can't hide from Him.

19

_____ - He is all powerful (Luke 1:37). He is strong and powerful enough to meet any situation in my life. Nothing is too hard for God, even if it seems impossible to us.

_____ - He never changes (Psalm 33:11). I can count on Him. I don't have to worry about Him changing His mind. His Word is the same yesterday, today and tomorrow.

_____ - He never lies (Psalm 33:4). He doesn't tell little lies or big lies. He doesn't speak half-truths. If He says something, we should believe it and act upon it, because what He is saying is truth.

Choose two or more of these attributes and explain what they mean or could mean in your life today.

_____

_____

_____

_____

_____

_____

_____

_____

Making it personal . . .

When you learn who God is and what His character is, and realize that He loves you, always tells the truth, and is a faithful friend, then you can trust Him completely with your life.

Have you dedicated your eyes to the Lord for His use? Are you able to say "Lord, I give you my eyes to be used for your honor and glory, and with your help I will keep my eyes on you and the things you consider important."

Like Job of old, make a covenant with your eyes, not to look upon any unclean thing (Job 31:1).

Making it prayerful . . .

Dear Lord, Help me to keep my eyes on you while I have limited vision so I won't be ashamed when I behold you face to face. Thank you, Lord for always telling me the truth even when I don't always want to hear it. You are trustworthy, loving and good Help my eyes to be truly beautiful so that when people look at them, they will see Jesus.

Chapter 3

Your Ears

What happens when we hear Satan's lie and believe it?

Beautiful ears listen to God and do what He says. If they just listen, they're not beautiful. They must listen and obey - the two go together!

Write out James 1:22_____
_____
_____

Write out Romans 2:13_____
_____
_____

Write out James 2:20_____
_____

Satan is a liar and the father of lies. He not only lies once in a while - he NEVER tells the truth, and we can NEVER trust him. When we listen to Satan's lies and believe them, we fall under God's judgment, and this happens whether we are believers or unbelievers. The only thing that keeps us sheltered from our enemy is to trust and obey God.

Unbelievers in Noah's day

What was the condition of the world in the days of Noah? (Genesis 6:5-7, 11-12)_____
_____
_____

How is the condition of the world today similar? Give some examples._____

_____

_____

_____

_____

How was Noah described in II Peter 2:5?

_____

Noah preached to the unbelievers of that day about the things of God. He would tell them that God's judgment was coming - "Repent and be saved; turn your life around; don't continue in the way you are going; stop before it's too late." God was warning people through the preaching of Noah. Did they hear - Yes! Did they obey - No!

What do you think God is saying to unbelievers today?

_____

At the same time that God was preaching His message through Noah, Satan was saying "Do your own thing and enjoy life. Don't worry about judgment." Satan is giving that same message to unbelievers today. Absolutely nothing has changed.

The people listened to Satan (the liar) instead of God. What does Matthew 24:38-39 tell us?

_____

_____

_____

_____

As Noah preached, the people continued to live their lives as usual. They were consumed with their day to day living and the pleasures of sin. They heard the message of righteousness, but they chose to dismiss it. And the very same thing is happening in our time.

God's judgment on the people in Noah's day is described in Genesis 7:23-24. _____

_____

_____

_____

When God says something, you can count on it! There is soon coming a time of judgment on earth for unbelievers described as The Tribulation. Take a look at Matthew 24:3-14 and list some things that will be happening in the first half:_____

_____

_____

_____

_____

_____

_____

_____

_____

_____

Matthew 24:21-29 describes the 2nd half of The Tribulation called The Great Tribulation. What do we learn about that time?_____

_____

_____

_____

_____

The Great Tribulation is going to be a time of horror for everyone who chooses evil over good, lies over truth. It's going to be a time when God's wrath is poured out upon all who refuse to believe Him and accept His free gift of eternal life which He purchased through the blood of His Son, Jesus Christ.

God speaks to us today and is warning us about that time through the Bible, evangelists, church, Christian television, the internet, radio, tracts, books, films and personal testimonies. Everyone will be without excuse. Just like in the days of Noah, Satan is very busy saying "Don't worry about it, you're okay, God won't judge you." And people are listening to the lie instead of the truth.

Then the Bible tells us about the ultimate judgment of all unbelievers. What does Revelation 20:11-15 tell us about that?_____

_____

_____

_____

God does not choose this for us. What does II Peter 3:9 tell us?_____

_____

The choice is ours. We can take the free gift that God holds out to us of eternal life through Jesus Christ, or we can choose destruction by listening to the deceitful voice of Satan. Who do you take your orders from? Who do you trust?

And what about believers who don't obey God - what happens to them? As Christians, we can never lose our salvation (John 10:27-30), but there are still consequences to pay for listening to Satan's voice and disobeying God.

Jonah, a believer who didn't obey

Jonah was a prophet of God, a preacher. He was preaching the same message that Noah did - "Repent. . . be saved . . . God's judgment is coming.

What did God tell Jonah to do? (Jonah 1:2)

_____

_____

Ninevah was a wicked city filled with sin. Jonah decided he didn't want to go because he didn't want the people of Ninevah to repent and be saved after all the evil they had done.

So what did Jonah do? (Jonah 1:3)

_____

_____

Jonah not only ran away, but he ran in the opposite direction of what God had called him to do. Do we sometimes see people as too wicked to accept Christ, and so we don't warn them about what is coming?

The Great Tribulation will be here sooner than any of us think. Yet we sit in our comfortable homes and church and have our fellowship just like nothing is going to happen, and we're not warning people!

Noah preached to a wicked people and not one was saved. But at least God's warning was heard and the people had a choice. We also need to make sure people have a chance to choose. Jonah set himself up as a pious judge, and decided that the people shouldn't have a choice because they were so wicked. How glad I am that we have a gracious and loving God who shows mercy to sinners and gives them many chances to repent.

Jonah, because of his disobedience and self-righteous attitude, fell under God's judgment. He heard what God wanted him to do and refused to do it. What was his judgment? (Jonah 1:17)

_____

_____

_____

Maybe you have a picture in your mind of something you saw in a children's book of Jonah sitting in a whale, maybe in a rocking chair, just sort of waiting it out quite comfortably. What does Jonah 2:1-7 tell you about what it was like for Jonah?_____

_____

_____

_____

_____

Jonah's judgment was designed by God to chasten Jonah for his disobedience to God's directive in his life and to cause him to repent and to do what God had called him to do regardless of his feelings about it.

What miracle did God perform when Jonah prayed? (Jonah 2:10)_____

_____

Jonah must have been quite a sight, bleached out by the acids in the fish's belly and coming to preach to the people in Ninevah.

What miracle did God perform in the city of Ninevah when Jonah did what he was supposed to do? (Jonah 3:5-10)

_____

_____

_____

_____

This was the greatest revival in history when an entire city turned to God!

Believers today

What does God tell us to do? (Matthew 28:19-20)

_____

_____

_____

What is your response to God? _____

We sometimes get so caught up in the busyness, pleasures and worries of life that we often don't make time to witness or warn people about the judgment that is coming. We get scared, we fear ridicule, and sometimes we just don't care.

What happens when believers don't obey God?
(I Corinthians 11:30-32)_____

_____

If you are a believer, you will never be condemned like the world, but you will be chastened by God, like a father chastens his child. Decide to listen to God who tells you the truth and wants the best for you, and then warn others about God's coming judgment. People's lives are in danger. People we know! We need to be warning them.

There was a great song many years ago sung by Steve Green called _People Need The Lord._ In that song it shares that we pass by people every day who are empty and filled with care and private pain. We see them laugh, but inside they are crying out for answers. The song challenges us to take God's light to a hurting world because people need the Lord. No cost is too great for sharing the message of hope with those who are lost.

That song should challenge us as Christians to remember what we were like before we came to know the Lord, and all that God has done for us since. Are we selfish enough to keep that message to ourselves, or concerned enough about others to introduce them to Jesus!

I am concerned for: _____
With God's help, I will pray for them and ask God for an opportunity to speak to them about their eternal salvation this week. Go with confidence, boldness, and a joyful heart. You have good news to share.

> *Lord, lay some soul upon my heart*
> *And love that soul through me;*
> *And may I nobly do my part*
> *To win that soul to thee*
> (author unknown)

Be aware that winning souls is in God's plan for your life. (Psalm 126)
Be aware that people are hurting and need the Lord.
Set aside time each week to tell people about the Lord (Ephesians 5:16)
Diligently prepare your heart to win souls. (Proverbs 16:1)
>Pray
>Write out your testimony
>Memorize Scripture
>Know how to lead a soul to Christ
>Pray for specific people
>Realize that God's Word is powerful

Have a definite plan and work hard at it (Ecclesiastes 9:10a)
>Write evangelistic letters
>Invite people to your home
>Give out tracts
>Share Christian books, magazines and movies
>Let people know you care

Invite people to church and life group every week.
>Give them a church bulletin
>Tell them about your life group/Sunday school class
>Offer to pick them up

Depend on God for results (I Corinthians 3:6-7)

Making it personal

Plan of salvation verses: (Write them out)

Romans 3:23_____

_____

Romans 6:23_____

_____

_____

Romans 5:8_____

_____

_____

John 3:16_____

_____

_____

_____

Romans 10:9_____

_____

_____

_____

Romans 10:13_____

_____

_____

Assurance of Salvation verses (write them out)

John 10:27-28_____

_____

_____

_____

_____

I John 5:11-13_____

_____

_____

_____

_____

_____

_____

_____

_____

Making it prayerful . . .

Dear Lord, so many voices call to me in this life and it can
be confusing at times. Thank you for your Word that
can cut through the confusion and save souls.
Thank you that you sent Jesus to take the penalty for
my sin and opened my eyes to your salvation.
Give me a burden for souls, dear Lord, and help me
to share your love and salvation with others.

Chapter 4

Your Ears
Listening to God who tells us the truth

The Bible describes God as our Shepherd, and describes us as sheep. Sheep, if left to themselves, would soon wander away from the flock and fall prey to ravenous wolves. The Shepherd is the only hope for the sheep. If they stay close enough to Him to listen to His voice, they won't be in any danger. It is only when they begin to move away from the Shepherd and go their own way that they get into trouble.

What does Isaiah 53:6 tell us?_____

_____

_____

_____

Three reasons why we should listen to and obey our Shepherd: *To know the truth, To acquire wisdom,* and *To avoid being deceived*

1. *To know the truth*
What do these verses tell us about truth?

Deuteronomy 32:4 -

_____

John 14:6 - _____

John 17:17 - _____

_____

My sheep hear my voice...

Conclusion: First we must have a personal relationship with Jesus Christ. Then we must listen to God's Word and obey it, for God cannot lie and His Word can be trusted.

2. *To acquire wisdom*

Wisdom is the one thing that everyone needs in order to cope with life. A good definition of wisdom is *living skillfully, judging rightly, and following the soundest course of action.*

We have decisions to make every day, and if we don't have the right basis on which to make those decisions, then we could make grave mistakes.

What does James 1:5 tell us?_____

_____

_____

What are at least eight benefits of wisdom found in Proverbs 3:13-18?

1. _____
2. _____
3. _____
4. _____
5. _____
6. _____
7. _____
8. _____

Conclusion: True wisdom comes from God and has many benefits. Therefore, we need to stay tuned in to God's Word, the Bible.

3. *To avoid being deceived*

No one wants to be known as a fool. If we listen to the voice of our Shepherd and obey it, we won't be deceived by Satan's lies. Satan is our #1 enemy and if he can't bring us down to hell with him, he will try to make us ineffective and defeated believers here on earth. He hates God and us.

What does I Peter 5:8 say about our enemy?

_____

_____

_____

If we are just hearers of the Word, and not doers, Satan will come along and twist what we have heard or make us forget what we have heard. He accomplishes this by:

John 8:44 - L_____

II Corinthians 4:4 - B_____ our M_____

Revelation 12:12 gives us the enemy's motive for stepping up his game. What do you think it is?

_____

Misery loves company. Satan knows he is the loser and that Jesus Christ is the winner.

Revelation 20:10 tells of his end:

_____

_____

The more time we spend in the Bible, listening to the words our Shepherd speaks, the less chance we have of following a counterfeit voice - the voice of the enemy.

If we live by the Words of our Shepherd, we don't have to worry that we are being deceived. We can trust our

Shepherd to protect us from all the evil outside the fold.

Jesus promises in Matthew 28:20 "Lo, I am with you always, even to the end of the age." He wants to guide your life and lead you into greener pastures than you've ever known before, or even imagined.

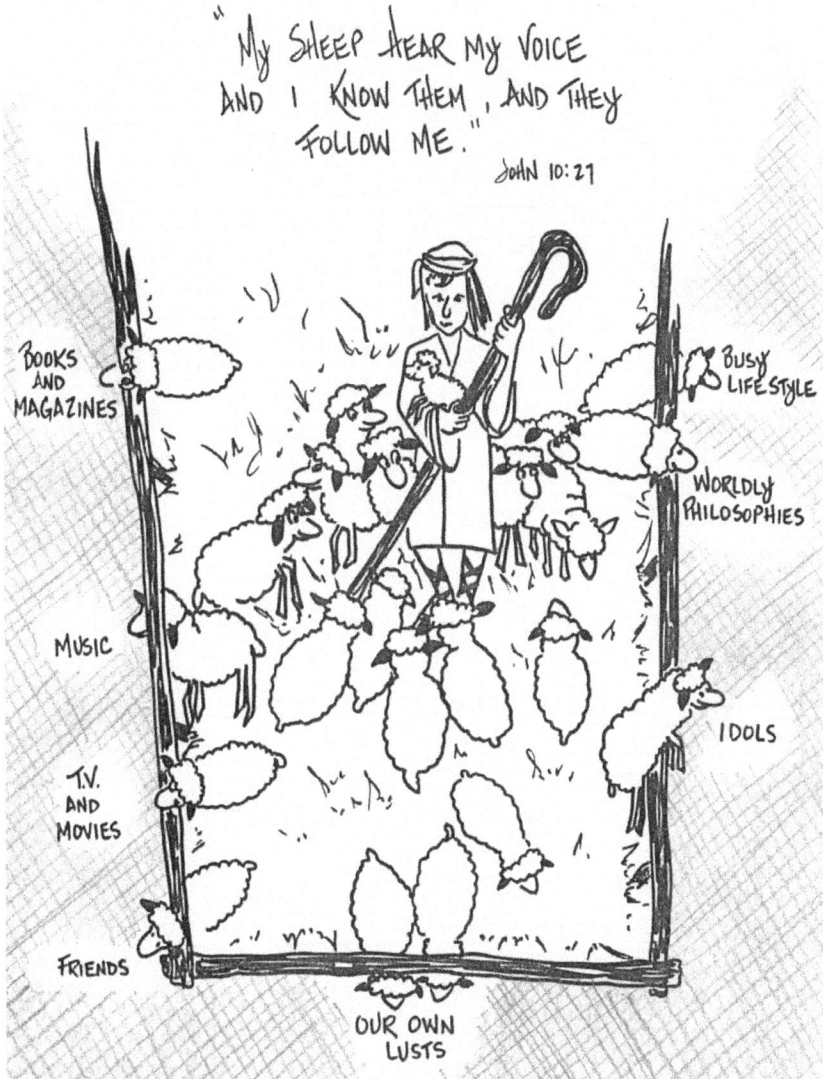

Artwork by Jackie Vebber

Making it personal . . .

Read Psalm 23 and write down and meditate on all the things you can think of that your Shepherd does for you.

Making it prayerful . . .

*Dear Lord, I thank you that you are the
Good shepherd who watches over and protects me.
Sometimes I act just like a dumb sheep and think
that I can do things my way without being hurt.
I start listening to other voices that contradict my
Shepherd and start to stray. Thank you for always
taking me back into the fold, and for your love and mercy.
Lord, help me to remember that you are truth, and that
only when I stay close to you will I be safe from the enemy.*

Chapter 5

Your Feet

Feet that walk the Broad Road

Just like the other parts of your body, your feet can either serve God or Satan. The Lord knew that you would have trouble with your feet, so He put this warning in His Word:

> *"Ponder the path of your feet,*
> *And let all your ways be established.*
> *Turn not to the right or the left;*
> *remove your foot from evil."*
> Proverbs 4:26-27

There are two choices our feet have - to walk on the Broad Road or the Narrow Road.

In this chapter we will look at feet that walked the Broad Road. They signed up for the grand tour, and their tour guide turned out to be none other than the great deceiver, Satan.

What does Matthew 7:13 tell us?_____

_____

_____

_____

_____

The enemy knows how to make bad things look good. First he puts a spotlight on the beginning of the tour and makes it easy for you to enter the Broad Road. Wealth, sex, religion, power and "do it my way" philosophies are enticingly displayed. He promises a low-cost, high-fun tour. What he doesn't tell you is that behind all those glamorous displays is darkness where we will stumble and fall and finally give way to our own destruction.

People choose the Broad Road because it has many interesting paths to follow and you will have lots of companionship along the way. The Broad Road promises to be exciting, with happiness and thrills beyond measure.

Because we are in such a hurry to get what we want, we listen without checking out the tour guide's credentials. We get swept up in the mad whirl of self-pleasure and doing things "our way."

In order to get a fresh dose of reality, let's look at some Bible people whose feet walked the Broad Road.

Judas Iscariot

Judas is, perhaps, the sorriest example of them all because he was right at the entrance to the Narrow Road until his feet deceived him by running over to the Broad Road where all the crowds were.

What was his motive? (Matthew 26:14-16)_____

He could have had all the riches Jesus had to offer, but he settled for temporary riches.

What is God's warning in Ecclesiastes 5:10?_____

_____

_____

_____

Wealth in itself is temporary and elusive. Only Jesus satisfies!

What did Judas do in his pursuit of money? (Matthew 26:47-49)

_____

Because of his love for money, Judas betrayed the only one who could bring satisfaction and lasting riches. For 30 pieces of silver, Judas betrayed the one who loved him and the one who came to give him life.

	Judas gained a few pieces of silver, but what did he lose? Unscramble the following words to find out. (The verses will give you a hint if you get stuck.)	
	OYJ	John 15:11; 16:22
	CAPEE	John 16:33
	COTFORM	II Corinthians 7:4
	HAULGING	Job 8:21
	GYROL	I Chronicles 16:27
	RHOON	I Chronicles 16:27
	SLENDSAG	I Chronicles 16:27
	THRENGTS	I Chronicles 16:27
	OVATSLAIN	Psalm 51:12
	DWISMO	Ecclesiastes 2:26
	GONS	Isaiah 30:29
	PHOE	Romans 15:13
	VOLE	Galatians 5:22
	YOHL SITRIP	Ephesians 5:18
	OGOD MANE	Proverbs 22:1
	GLON FILE	Proverbs 3:2
	CHERIS	Proverbs 22:4
	WONCR	Proverbs 4:9

Judas lost out on all that for 30 pieces of silver. Satan sure gave Judas a bad deal, but then, that's Satan's game - to deceive!

Where did the Broad Road lead Judas? (Matthew 27:3-5)

_____

Satan promised him wealth, but instead led him on a path of sin that led to depression, which in turn led to suicide.

He still works like that today. The enemy does not want us to have hope. He wants to destroy us.

What do you think Judas could have done differently after betraying Jesus that might have changed his situation? (see Matthew 4:17; I John 1:9)

_____

Jezebel

Read through I Kings, chapters 18, 19 and 21. There you will find Jezebel's motive for signing up for the Broad Road. What are your thoughts on this?_____
_____
_____

I believe her motive involved greed and power which led to violence. Jezebel lived a violent life and died a violent death. There is nothing about her that is attractive. She had no regard for others as she pursued what she wanted from life.

God sent His prophets into the world to bring light to the people through His Word. John 3:20 tells us why Jezebel didn't respond to God's prophets. Write out that verse.

_____
_____
_____

Sum up what the following verses say about the evil things that Jezebel did?

I Kings 18:13_____

I Kings 19:1-3_____

I Kings 21:5-16_____
_____

I Kings 21:25_____

The Broad Road led Jezebel to her demise. Describe her death. (I Kings 21:23; II Kings 9:33-37)

_____

_____

_____

What a bitter end! All that was found of her was her skull, her feet, and the palms of her hands. Satan promised her power, but delivered a horrible death. What you sow, you will reap, and this woman sowed violence all throughout her life.

Scribes and Pharisees

These were the religious leaders and teachers in the Temple. What was their motive in signing up for the Broad Road? (Matthew 23:5-7)

_____

"Religion" is a system of good works designed to obtain the favor of God. This is how Satan tells people to find their way to God. The religious leaders had not only bought into that philosophy, but were leading the people of their congregation astray. They were "puffed up" in their own importance.

What does God warn us about in Ephesians 2:8-9?

_____

_____

_____

Religion puts the emphasis on man and not on God. The Bible teaches that the emphasis is on God and not man. Completely opposite views.

Write out Romans 3:10_____

Write out Romans 3:11_____
_____

Christ has done it all, and the only way we can come to God and receive eternal life is to receive Christ as our personal Savior. He died on the cross and shed His blood to pay for our sins, and was made righteousness for us. He is the perfect Lamb of God who came to take away the sins of the world. No one can get to Heaven by their own merit.

The religious leaders did not believe this, however, and instead, preached salvation through law-keeping and doing good works. They deceived themselves and others by not believing the truth when it was told them. Jesus called them hypocrites in Matthew 23 because their walk did not match their talk. They were saying one thing but doing another.

What did Jesus say they were really like in Matthew 23:27-28?_____
_____
_____
_____
_____
_____

Where did the Broad Road lead the religious leaders? (Luke 19:47-48)_____
_____

Can you picture it? Here are all these pious so-called "good" religious leaders who were supposed to be examples to the people. They were so concerned about God's Law, yet they sought to put Jesus (God's Son) to death. They missed it entirely!

Religious on the outside, but rotten on the inside. And even today there are some people who would rather stick with their religion of good works, than admit that they are sinners. Religion does not earn you a place in Heaven. Only a relationship with Jesus Christ will get you there.

Shechem

We read Shechem's story in Genesis 34. What do you think his motive was for being on the Broad Road?

_____

This is a young man who was ruled by sexual pleasure instead of exercising self-control and respect for women.

God's warning in Ephesians 5:5:_____

_____

_____

_____

Dinah, the daughter of Jacob, was out walking and caught Shechem's eye. What did Shechem do? (Genesis 34:1-2)

_____

God doesn't have anything against sex – He invented it! But there are rules concerning it. What does Hebrews 13:4 say?_____

_____

_____

Instead of waiting for marriage, Shechem took what he wanted because he thought he was entitled.

How did Shechem feel about Dinah after his unlawful act? (Genesis 34:3-4)

_____

It's too bad Shechem didn't try to get to know Dinah first and wait until after marriage for the sexual act. Instead

Shechem was about to find out the hard way that God hates sin.

Where did the Broad Road lead Shechem? (Read all of Genesis 34, and find answer from verse 26)

_____

_____

Satan tempted Shechem with sexual sin, but delivered instead deceit and death.

There are many more Bible characters we could study, showing how Satan deceived them into thinking they could do whatever they wanted, and that there would be no price to pay . . . but I think you get the idea. Satan is a liar!

Besides all the gruesome things that can happen to people on the Broad Road, the worst is yet to come: The Great White Throne Judgment when the dead, great and small, will stand before God, and their names will not be found in the Book of Life. They will spend eternity in the lake of fire because they trusted in Satan instead of God.

Making it Personal . . .

Write out Proverbs 14:12_____

_____

_____

What has Satan tempted you with? Is there something in your life that you need to confess to the Lord as sin and then forsake. When you do that it is called repentance, and you will receive forgiveness.

A good definition of repentance is found in Psalm 38:17-18: *"I am ready to stop. I am sorrowful. I am ready to agree with God about my sin. I will turn my back on my sin."*

You can't claim I John 1:9 flippantly. God sees your heart. He knows when you are sorrowful and grieving over sin or when you're just trying to get off the hook for a while before you start regarding sin in your heart again. It's better to be honest with God and ask Him to take the desire from you, then pretend you're all right when you're not.

Making it Prayerful . . .

Dear Lord, thank you for the warnings in Your Word about the things I should avoid. Thank you for the examples you give of people who listened to the enemy and went down a wrong path when he presented sin as glamorous and exciting. Remind me often, Lord, that Satan is a liar, and help me to follow your direction for my life so that I can continue to run the race and arrive safely at the finish line - my eternal destination. I desire to finish well.

Chapter 6

Your Feet
Feet that walk the Narrow Road where God leads

Often when we think of "narrow" we think of restricting. We think that if we choose to walk on that road we're not going to have any fun and we'll have to live by a bunch of rules that will make us unhappy. Because we allow that doubt to take root in our heart, we make a hassle out of something that can be a beautiful joyful tour.

Remember . . . everyone on the Broad Road is headed for destruction. It doesn't matter how much fun it looks like they're having along the way. That's why the Bible calls them fools - they are laughing all the way to their own destruction. They walk and laugh through life, thinking they are getting away with something, yet the road is eventually going to come to an abrupt end and they're going to fall off into eternal darkness and torment. (Revelation 21:11-15)

Today's footprints are tomorrow's pathways.
Be careful where you step.

Beautiful feet walk the Narrow Road where God leads. What does Psalm 40:2 tell us?

_____

_____

_____

_____

If you have received Christ as your personal Savior, He has taken you off the path of destruction and placed your feet on the path of life.

If we keep on this pathway and walk with the light God gives us, we will eventually come out into a beautiful land. We will have everything we need and we will live forever joyful with the person who provided it all. How does Revelation 21:4 describe this place?_____

_____

_____

_____

God is going to bring us out into a perfect land where we will have joy forevermore.

The Bible has much to say about the way we should walk the Narrow Road in order to get to our destination in the best possible shape.

$$\approx \textit{We should walk in the light} \approx$$
I John 1:7

When we walk in the light, what two things will we have according to I John 1:7?_____

_____

These two things are necessary if we're going to have a joyful trip. Fellowship is important because we can talk, and share, and sing along the way, and friendships grow sweet. Then, if we do fall at some point, God forgives us, and our friends help pick us up and get us started again. It's a team effort - we're not all by ourselves.

On the Broad Road, even though there are many more people on that road, the fellowship is not as sweet because everyone is trying to go their own way and do things to bring glory to themselves. Sometimes they walk right over you instead of stopping to help you because their first concern is themselves and the things they are chasing after.

Forgiveness of sins is very important also because when

we sin, we walk in darkness. When we ask the Lord to forgive our sins, we can continue to walk in light. It is a necessity to have forgiveness of sin so that God can continue to light our pathway.

What does Psalm 119:105 tell us?

_____

_____

It's important to study and obey God's Word if we want a well-lit pathway where we won't stumble and trip. God gives us enough light to walk step by step each day.

What does the psalmist ask God for in Psalm 119:133?

_____

_____

In other words, "As I look into your Word, God, shine light on my path so that I can see clearly the way I should go and not get caught up in sin." This is a prayer all of us could benefit from.

In our day by day walk, we're to go to God's Word to find out the right way to go. When we do this, we won't be taking side roads and detours that will mess us up. God's Word tells us what direction to take and provides us with light so that we can see where we're going.

Can you imagine driving your car at night without headlights? Yet this is sometimes what we do in our Christian life as we go on our journey. The more we use the light and follow directions, the easier our trip will be. Otherwise, we will wind up lost until we find our way back or someone comes and finds us and brings us back.

What does II Timothy 2:15 exhort us to do?

_____

_____

_____

The next time your pastor says you should be in the Word daily, the next time your Bible teacher tells you to memorize Scripture, the next time a friend exhorts you to live the Christian life . . . realize that this is the way God gives you more light so that you can get further ahead in your Christian walk and draw closer to your destination. Don't harden your heart. Be thankful for the light God gives you.

≈ *We should walk humbly* ≈
Micah 6:8

Walking humbly means:

1. *In the fear of the Lord* - Acts 9:31

Write out the following verses:

Proverbs 1:7_____

_____

_____

Proverbs 3:7_____

_____

Proverbs 8:13a_____

Fear of the Lord means trusting and respecting God for who He is and for lighting your pathway. It also means developing a hatred for evil; a hatred for that darkness that keeps trying to suck you in and get you lost. Ask the Lord to help you to hate sin. Sin is deceitful - it may look harmless and pleasurable, but it will turn on you without warning.

2. *Walk in Christ*

Write out Colossians 2:6_____

_____

_____

Walking in Christ means being dead to sin and alive unto God. Saying no to darkness and yes to light. Being aware of "What Jesus would have you do," instead of following your own natural inclinations. It doesn't mean you will never sin again, but it does mean that you will be unhappy if you continue in sin.

3. Walk by the Spirit

Write out Galatians 5:16_____

_____

_____

The Holy Spirit of God leads us into all truth. When the Word of God indwells us richly, when we make it our focus in life, we will have light to make good decisions.

How do we know we are filled with the Spirit according to Ephesians 5:19-21?

We will be speaking in . . .

We will be singing and . . .

We will be giving . . .

We will be submitting ourselves to . . .

These things will be in your heart and characterize your life if you are walking in the Spirit. Do they characterize your life? If not, what do you need to do to get back on track?

"Happiness is a choice!" You should have an attitude of excitement and expectation as God leads you on the Narrow Road journey.

≈ <u>We should walk worthy</u> ≈

Write out Colossians 1:10

_____
_____
_____
_____

Unto all pleasing

> Peaceable - Romans 12:18
>> Not trying to stir up arguments and strife. Not always trying to be right. Gentle with people.

> Honest - Romans 12:17
>> Not trying to deceive people in any way. Not acting like a hypocrite. Everything we do should be out in the open.

> Kind - Romans 12:10
>> Realize that the people traveling with you on the Narrow Road are your brothers and sisters in Christ. They are your family and it is your responsibility to love them and treat them with kindness.

Being fruitful in every good work

Write out John 15:5,8_____

_____
_____
_____
_____
_____
_____

We should be continually producing fruit for the glory of God.

Lord, help me to abide in you,
    for I know you are the Vine.
The only way to live and grow
    is to keep my hand in thine.
Help me to produce much fruit,
    and be bountiful for Thee,
And I will give you all the praise
    for what you've done for me.

Are You Fruitful?

The following types of fruit should be produced in our lives as Christians. <u>Look up the verses and write them out.</u>

Fruit of the Spirit

This fruit comes by letting the Holy Spirit control our lives, resulting in godly character qualities being produced in us.

Galatians 5:22,23 _____

_____

_____

_____

Fruit of Righteousness

This fruit comes by letting Christ live His life through us.

Philippians 1:11 _____

_____

_____

Fruit of Soulwinning

Making sure that people know they have a choice of getting off the Broad Road of destruction and getting on the Narrow Road that leads to eternal life. Seeking to win the lost by introducing them to Jesus Christ.

Proverbs 11:30_____

_____

Fruit of our lips

Giving thanks to God in all things. Trusting Him to work all things for our good. Praising God in all situations.

Hebrews 13:15_____

_____

_____

_____

First fruits

Honoring the Lord by giving our best, not just what we have left over.

Proverbs 3:9_____

_____

_____

Fruit of good works

This is a combination of all the other fruits and results in bringing glory to God.

Matthew 5:16_____

_____

_____

_____

We cannot produce fruit on our own. We need to be attached to the life-giving vine, Jesus Christ. Only then can we produce fruit in abundance.

We also walk worthy by *Increasing in the knowledge of God*

Write out Proverbs 9:9

_____

_____

_____

Learn more each day about God and grow in faith. Don't be satisfied with what you already know, but desire to learn more and more about God.

Making it Personal . . .

In speaking of beautiful feet, we cannot forget Romans 10:15 which says:
> *"How beautiful are the feet of them*
> *that preach the gospel of peace*
> *and bring glad tidings of good things."*

Have you dedicated your feet to the Lord for His use? Are you planting them firmly on the Narrow Road and following that road from the light of God's Word? Are you learning to walk humbly in Christ by letting the Holy Spirit guide you? Do you walk worthy, and are others able to see that God is producing fruit in your life? Talk with God about this.

Making it Prayerful . . .

Dear Lord, thank you for taking me off the Broad Road
which leads to destruction and for establishing my
goings on the Narrow Path.
Help me to always humbly walk in the light, and to be
a light to others who need to find their way.
As I follow You, I pray that fruit would be produced
in me for Your honor and glory.

Chapter 7

Your Mouth
Speaking Foolishly

Proverbs 10:20 says in essence "When a good man speaks, he is worth listening to, but the words of fools are a dime a dozen." We need to pray that when we open our mouth to speak, our words will be worth listening to.

A foolish mouth is characterized by:
Quickness of speech
A deceitful tongue
Murmuring and complaining

The following are Biblical examples of people who had foolish mouths

Nabal - I Samuel 25 - Quickness of Speech
Root cause - Pride

How does the Bible describe Nabal? I Samuel 25:2-3

_____

_____

David, Israel's next king, had protected Nabal's sheep and men against robbers and other perils. Now David and his men needed food. David sent his servants to Nabal to respectfully appeal to him for food. What was Nabal's arrogant reply to that request? I Samuel 25:10-11

_____

_____

_____

How did Nabal's reply affect David? I Samuel 25:13

_____

_____

What does Proverbs 15:1 tell us about Nabal's answer and David's response?_____

_____

_____

Although Nabal spoke arrogantly regarding David's request, he had a beautiful wife named Abigail who was gracious and saved her husband from David's wrath. What happened when Abigail told Nabal she had given food to David and his men? I Samuel 25:37

_____

_____

How did God deal with Nabal? I Samuel 25:38

_____

Nabal took full credit and responsibility for his prosperity, instead of thanking God for His good hand upon his life, and humbly sharing with those in need.

What have you personally learned about quickness of speech from this story that you can apply to your life?

_____

_____

_____

_____

Haman – Book of Esther – A Deceitful Tongue
Root cause - Hate

Haman practiced deceit and flattery to get what he wanted and was not a man of integrity. What started Haman's plot of revenge on Mordecai, the Jew? Esther 3:1-5

_____

_____

_____

Being a Jew, the only one Mordecai would bow down to was The Most High God. Haman was infuriated because he wanted people to bow down to him as if he were God! His hatred for those who wouldn't caused him to have an evil desire. What was it? Esther 3:6

_____

_____

Haman went to King Ahasuerus, flattering him, and telling the king about a people who would not obey the King's laws. What was Haman's suggestion to the King? Esther 3:8-9

_____

_____

What effect did the King's decree have on Mordecai and the Jewish people? Esther 4:1-3

_____

_____

_____

Haman's mouth had dealt treacherously with God's people. However, he had not counted on one thing - God's sovereignty. God was still in control and used Esther, the Queen, to defeat this scheme because she was a Jewess.

How did King Ahasuerus feel about Esther? Esther 2:17

_____

_____

Haman didn't have a chance! When we set ourselves up as God, we let ourselves in for many frustrations and ultimate defeat.

When Esther was told about Haman's plot against the Jews what did she do? Esther 4:15-17 _____

_____

Esther 5:9-13 tells about Haman's boasting to his friends about his high position and honors. But even this does not bring lasting satisfaction. Why?_____

_____

What did Haman do because of advice from his wife and friends? Esther 5:14

_____

Haman's lofty ideas were toppled by a king's insomnia. When the king couldn't sleep, he had someone read to him out of the book of history, and it was found out that Mordecai had once saved the king's life and had never been rewarded for it.

What was Haman forced to do? How was he humbled? Esther 6:6-12_____

_____

_____

Queen Esther held a private banquet for the King and Haman. What was her purpose? Esther 7:1-6

_____

_____

Finally, because of Haman's mouth which spoke against God's anointed people with disdain and deceit, Haman met his death. How was this accomplished? Esther 7:10

_____

_____

What have you learned about a deceitful tongue from this story that you can apply to your life?_____

_____

_____

_____

_____

Miriam and Aaron - Numbers 12 - Murmuring and Complaining
Root Cause: Ungratefulness

This is the story of a brother-sister conflict. Moses was the brother of Miriam and Aaron. Instead of upholding Moses in prayer, knowing that he was God's man, they used their mouths to murmur and complain against Moses.

What were Miriam and Aaron upset about, and who heard their complaining? Numbers 12:1-2

_____

_____

Both Miriam and Aaron knew that Moses was special in God's eyes. In Exodus we see Miriam as a young girl in Egypt. A decree had gone out from Pharoah stating that every Hebrew baby boy would be killed. Miriam's mother gave birth to a baby boy and hid him for 3 months so he would be safe. When she could no longer hide him, what did she do? Exodus 2:3_____

_____

_____

_____

In Exodus 2:4-6, what special event happened that Miriam witnessed?_____

_____

_____

What showed Miriam's love for Moses? Exodus 2:7-8

_____

_____

_____

Because of these events, Miriam knew full well that God had a special plan for Moses.

Aaron also knew that God had chosen Moses to be a great leader and that he was to be his helper. Exodus 4:15-16 tells of the relationship God wanted them to have with each other. Explain the following diagram in relation to these verses:

God → Moses → Aaron

_____

_____

_____

_____

Aaron saw all the awesome miracles that God did through Moses in the land of Egypt. But even knowing and seeing all these things, both Miriam and Aaron spoke against Moses.

In Numbers 12:6-8, how did God put Moses above all the other prophets, and what question did he ask Miriam and Aaron?_____

_____

_____

_____

_____

What did God do to Miriam for speaking against Moses? Numbers 12:10-15

_____

_____

_____

According to I Timothy 2:12, why might God's judgment have been stricter on Miriam?

_____

_____

_____

What does it say in Numbers 12:11 that would make you think that Aaron repented and was therefore spared a harsh judgment?

_____

What have you learned about a murmuring and complaining mouth from this story that can apply to your life?_____

_____

_____

_____

_____

Are there any authorities/leaders in your life that you need to be praying for instead of complaining about?

_____

Making it Personal . . .

Think about your mouth - your tongue, your words. Are you bringing glory to God or are you speaking foolishly?

Are you quick to speak because of pride? Do you need to think before you speak and ask for wisdom?

Is your tongue deceitful? Are you hiding hatred in your heart? Do you build others up or tear them down?

Do you find yourself murmuring and complaining because of ungratefulness towards God and others? Are you covering up envy or are you thankful for what God gives you?

Making it Prayerful . . .

_Dear Lord, I thank you for the warnings in Your Word
about the foolish tongue. Help me not to give quick
answers, and think I know everything, but to take time to
ask you for wisdom. Help me not to tear other people
down, but to appreciate and encourage each person
because you love them. And Lord, help me not to murmur
and complain, but in everything I do may I have a heart of
thanksgiving and sing praises to your Name. Amen._

Chapter 8

Your Mouth
Speaking With God's Wisdom

Time after time God's Word warns us about the use of our mouth. How is the tongue described in James 3:8?

_____

We need to learn how to control this part of our body so that it won't get loose to harm anyone. What does James 3:10 say about your mouth?

_____

_____

_____

With God in control, you will replace cursing with praise. Your lips will curve into smiles of love, and your tongue will be used to build people up instead of tearing them down.

Write out Psalm 19:14 and make this your daily prayer:

A beautiful mouth is slow to speak

"Wherefore, my beloved brethren, Let every man be swift to hear, <u>slow to speak</u>, slow to wrath
James 1:19

When we answer a matter quickly, we are speaking in arrogance and pride instead of asking God for wisdom, and waiting for His answer.

Being slow to speak shows we have:

W_____ - Proverbs 10:19

H_____ - Proverbs 27:2

L_____ - Romans 12:10

Sometimes we are so busy talking and voicing our opinions, we have no time to listen to that still small voice of God.

What does Proverbs 10:19 say?_____

_____

_____

Ecclesiastes 5:2?_____

_____

_____

_____

_____

Turn to James 3:14-16 and write down things that characterize worldly wisdom when we are quick to speak.

_____   _____

_____   _____

_____   _____

_____   _____

It is so important to pause and pray before opening your mouth.

A beautiful mouth edifies others (builds them up)

"She opens her mouth with wisdom, and in her tongue is the law of kindness."
Proverbs 31:26

This verse is talking about the virtuous woman, and when we read it, it should fill us with a longing to become like her. I think most of us can look back with regret and sadness on times we have spoken with harshness and have hurt the feelings of those we love.

The virtuous woman has a beautiful mouth, and when she speaks, she has the welfare of others in mind. She only says things that build people up, teaching and instructing them with love.

Ephesians 4:29 is another great verse about edifying others. What does it tell us?

_____

_____

_____

_____

Besides hurting other people, who do we grieve when we tear people down? Ephesians 4:30

_____

What are we to put away? Ephesians 4:31

_____

_____

How should we act towards others, and why? Ephesians 4:32_____

_____

_____

_____

65

List the 8 characteristics of wisdom that come from God in James 3:17:

_____   _____

_____   _____

_____   _____

_____   _____

A beautiful mouth praises God

"Because thy lovingkindness is better than life,
my lips shall praise thee."
Psalm 63:3

Singing praises to God shows that we are:
Thankful - Psalm 98:1
Joyful - Psalm 9:2
Obedient - I Thessalonians 5:18

I Thessalonians 5:18 tells us in what circumstances we should be praising God. What are they and why?

_____

_____

Now let's be practical about this. Why should we praise Him in everything? Romans 8:28

_____

_____

_____

No matter what happens to us in this life, our loving heavenly Father has promised to bring good out of it for us. He promises, and He cannot lie, so if we trust in His promise, we are free to praise Him regardless of our circumstances.

There is so much to praise God for, and here is your opportunity to do that right now. (See page 67)

**God's Provision
Is Abundant
I love thee, O Lord,
and Sing Praises
to Thy Name.**

Dear Heavenly Father,
I want to thank you for _____

_____

_____

_____

_____

_____

_____

_____

_____

_____

_____

I also want to tell you _____

_____

_____

_____

_____

Love,

Making it personal . . .

How does your mouth rate in the area of spiritual beauty? Do you really listen to what is being said or do you jump right in and voice your opinions and judgments before the whole story is told? Do you take time to pause and pray before you speak?

Do you edify others with your words? Are you kind and loving? Do you speak the truth in love? Or do you allow prejudice or jealousy to influence your thoughts and words?

Do you find things to praise God for each day, regardless of your circumstances? Do you trust God when He promises to work all things for your good? Do you think God is good?

Making it prayerful . . .

Dear Lord, help me to learn how to control my mouth. Help me to be slow to speak and to take the time to pause and pray first. Help me to be like the virtuous woman who opened her mouth with wisdom and kindness. How I long to be that beautiful, and so often I completely fail at it. And Lord, most of all, help me to have a thankful heart and to praise you for all you have done and are doing in my life.
"Let the words of my mouth, and the meditation of my heart, be acceptable in your sight, O Lord, my strength and my Redeemer." Amen.

Chapter 9

Your Heart
Unproductive Soil of the Uncultivated Heart

You may be absolutely gorgeous on the outside, but if your heart isn't beautiful, your outward beauty will fade! Whatever is in your heart will eventually make its way to the surface. You must be willing to turn your heart over to God so that He can give it an extreme beauty makeover.

What does God tell us in Jeremiah 24:7?

_____

_____

_____

_____

_____

We are going to be looking at The Parable of the Sower and the Seed in Matthew 13:3-23. In this parable we find the following terms and their definitions:

> Sower = God
> Soil = human hearts
> Seed = Word of God

We also find 3 types of uncultivated hearts - the callous heart, the careless heart and the cramped heart. Let's begin by looking at each one individually.

The Callous Heart – Matthew 13:4, 19
"And when He sowed, some of the seed fell along the path, and the birds came and ate it up."

"When anyone hears the word of the Kingdom
and does not understand it, the evil one
comes and snatches away what was sown in
his heart. This is the seed sown along the path."

According to the dictionary, what does callous mean?

_____

When the seed falls upon the path where everyone walks, it doesn't get into the soil, so the birds are able to come and eat the seed on top of the hard ground. This soil is so hard, it would probably take dynamite to break it up.

Characteristics of the "Callous Heart"
- Doesn't care about things of God
- Doesn't yield soil for Gardener's use
- Hard and insensitive

Proverbs 29:1 has a warning for those with callous hearts. What is it?_____

_____

_____

A Biblical example of a "Callous Heart" is Pharoah in Exodus 7-14. Pharoah probably had one of the most callous hearts ever. He heard the words of the Lord, but refused to obey them.

What did God say to Pharoah through Moses? Exodus 5:1

_____

_____

What was Pharoah's reply? Exodus 5:2

_____

_____

_____

_____

Pharoah had ten chances (10 sticks of dynamite) to have the hard ground of his callous heart broken up so that the seed of the Word of God could get in. God used plagues to get his attention. Look up the following Scriptures and write what the plague was.

Exodus 7:20-21 - Plague of b_____

Exodus 8:1-4 - Plague of f_____

Exodus 8:17 - Plague of g_____ (lice)

Exodus 8:24 - Plague of f_____

Exodus 9:6 - Plague on l_____

Exodus 9:10-11 - Plague of b_____

Exodus 9:23-26 - Plague of h_____

Exodus 10:13-15 - Plague of l_____

Exodus 10:22-23 - Plague of d_____

Exodus 11:5-6 - Plague on the f_____

Pharoah kept hardening his heart more and more, and then God hardened it even further. There comes a time when we are willfully sinning against God, that the Lord cuts us off and there is no chance for us to repent.

Finally, after all these plagues happened, Pharoah decided to let God's people go! He summoned Moses and Aaron during the night and said in Exodus 12:31:

_____

_____

_____

_____

Wow! A callous heart finally broken! Or was it? . . . . .
What were the second thoughts of Pharoah in Exodus
14:5b?

_____

_____

What did he do? Exodus 14:9

_____

_____

_____

_____

God finally had enough with Pharoah and Proverbs 29:1
was about to become a reality in Pharoah's life.

Summarize the miracle that happened in Exodus 14:21-22

_____

_____

_____

What final thing did God do to the Egyptians when they
tried to follow the Israelites across on dry land? Exodus
14:26-30

_____

_____

_____

_____

Pharoah lost his whole kingdom, but the ultimate
consequence in Pharoah's life was that he went into
eternity without knowing God personally.

God might be speaking to you right now, warning you that
you need to be sensitive to His Word and soften your heart
so that the Word can get into that soil and grow. If you
ignore God's warning, the seed is going to continue to land
on that hard ground and never take root because the birds

are going to come along and carry them away. And your heart will remain hard until you go into eternity without God.

The Careless Heart – Matthew 13:5-6; 13:20-21
"Some fell on rocky places where it did not have much soil. It sprang up quickly because the soil was shallow. But when the sun came up, the plants were scorched, and they withered because they had no root."

"The one who received the seed that fell on rocky places is the one who hears the word and at once receives it with joy. But since he has no root, he lasts only a short time. When trouble or persecution comes because of the word, he quickly falls away."

According to the dictionary, what does careless mean?

_____

_____

Characteristics of a "Careless Heart":
- Receives God's Word gladly, but only on a surface level
- Won't let God's Word get roots in deep
- Is offended when tribulation comes
- Hearer of the Word, and not a doer

This type of person may deceive themselves and others, but they don't deceive God. What does I Samuel 16:7b tell us?

_____

_____

A Biblical example of a "Careless Heart" is Saul in I Samuel 15. God gave Saul specific orders, and although Saul heard the Word of the Lord, he decided not to obey it completely. He would learn that incomplete obedience is not obedience at all.

What did the Lord tell Saul to do in I Samuel 15:3?

_____

_____

_____

_____

The Amalekites were ferocious enemies of God's chosen people, and in every generation fought against Israel from the days of Moses to the days of David.

How did Saul disobey? I Samuel 15:9_____

_____

_____

_____

What was Saul's excuse for not obeying? I Samuel 15:21,24_____

_____

_____

Saul, along with the people, made a deliberate choice to disobey God because they thought they knew better than God.

In I Samuel 15:22, what is a great truth that is made known?_____

God does not need our sacrifices, for Jesus is the perfect sacrifice. God requires our obedience.

In I Samuel 15:23a it tells what was in Saul's heart. No one could see it except the Lord because we can fool people, but cannot hide anything from God. What did Godsee?

_____

According to John 14:15, what proves that Saul did not really love God?

_____

What was the consequence in Saul's life when he rejected what God had to say? I Samuel 15:23b

_____

God had great plans for Saul. He allowed him to be the King of Israel, yet God wanted an obedient person. When Saul chose to go his own way and disobey God, then God rejected him and raised up another in his place.

Saul was good looking, talented, popular, yet all these things counted for nothing because he didn't put God first.

You might have everything going for you, but if you start disregarding God's Word, it doesn't matter who you are or how much you've got going for you. God will raise up another in your place.

The Cramped Heart – Matthew 13:7; 13:22
"Other seeds fell among thorns, which grew up and choked the plants."

"The one who received the seed that fell among the thorns is the one who hears the word, but the worries of this life and the deceitfulness of wealth choke it, making it unfruitful."

What is the dictionary definition of cramped?

_____

Characteristics of the "Cramped Heart":
- Cares of this world and deceitfulness of riches choke the Word of God
- Is unfruitful

What are some cares of this world that might choke the Word of God in your life? What are some things you are anxious about?

_____

_____

Why do you think riches are deceitful? _____

_____

_____

_____

Some think the things of this world are more important than spiritual (eternal) things. They have what we commonly call "tunnel vision" - they don't see the big picture. And when God tries to sow His Word in their heart, it is pricked by a thorn and dies.

What commandment is stated in I John 2:15?

_____

_____

What is the reason we should not love the world? I John 2:17_____

_____

_____

What does James 4:14b tell us?

_____

_____

_____

There are times we get so caught up in selfishly living our own lives that we often forget what is really important.

A Biblical example of a "Cramped Heart" is the Rich Young Ruler in Matthew 19:16-26.

Why did he come to Jesus? Matthew 19:16

_____

What was the first requirement that Jesus gave him?
Matthew 19:17-19

_____

Was this a problem to the young man? Matthew 19:20

_____

Then Jesus went to the heart of the matter. He knew what
the rich young ruler was harboring in his heart, and
challenged him in verse 21 to do 3 things. What were they?

        <u>S</u>_____ your possessions
        <u>G</u>_____ to the poor
        <u>C</u>_____ and <u>f</u>_____ Me

Did the young man pass or fail this test? Why? Matthew
19:22

_____

_____

What does Matthew 6:24 tell us?

_____

Jesus knew that this rich young ruler was giving his riches
first place in his life. They were so important to him that he
would even turn down eternal life for the pleasures he could
have now. How sad.

Summarize in your own words the warning I John 2:15-17
gives us regarding our possessions?

_____

_____

_____

_____

The consequence in the rich young ruler's life was that he lost out on eternal life for temporary pleasure. From a place of torment he's thinking back to that time when Jesus spoke to him personally and told him how to have eternal life, but the deceitfulness of riches hindered him. All his riches profit him nothing now, and he realizes he was deceived. He will live with regret for all eternity.

Making it Personal . . .

The "callous" heart, the "careless" heart and the "cramped" heart all prove the truth of Jeremiah 17:9. Write out this verse:_____
_____
_____

What does Proverbs 4:23 tell you to do?
_____
_____

In light of this what decision do you need to make today?
_____
_____
_____

Take some time to examine your heart. Is there anything that keeps you from surrendering your heart and life to Jesus? Can you be honest enough to say what it is to yourself and to God?
_____
_____
_____
_____

Making it Prayerful . . .

Dear Lord, we've seen how Pharoah hardened his heart to your word and arrogantly pursued his own agenda. We saw Saul obey you in some things, but it was not a complete obedience as he chose some of your word to disobey. And then we saw the rich young ruler who was a good man but harbored the deceitfulness of riches in his heart, and made them his focus.

Lord, help me to examine my own heart to see if there are things there that need to be removed that hinder me from trusting and obeying you completely. If I were to die today, would I have eternal life? If I were to die today, what would I regret?
Lord, you know my heart, and I pray you will reveal it to me in truth and love. Amen.

Chapter 10

Your Heart

Productive Soil of the Cultivated Heart

In this lesson we're going to look at the beautiful heart we should all desire to have. If your heart isn't beautiful, it doesn't matter how good you look on the outside for that beauty is fleeting. God can take an uncultivated heart, clean it up and make it the home of the Holy Spirit.

The Cultivated Heart – Matthew 13:8,23
"Still other seed fell on good soil, where it produced a crop - a hundred, sixty or thirty times what was sown."

"But the one who received the seed that fell on good soil is the man who hears the word and understands it. He produces a crop, yielding a hundred, sixty or thirty times what was sown."

According to the dictionary, what does cultivated mean?

_____
_____
_____

God is able to take this type of heart and convert it, making it a place for development and growth, producing a large amount of crops where there was nothing before.

Characteristics of the "Cultivated Heart"
- Listens to the Word of God
- Understands the Word of God
- Obeys the Word of God
- Is fruitful

Is Christ Comfortably at Home in your Heart?

A Christian's heart is like a house. As Jesus enters the house and goes through each of the rooms, this is what He finds:

The Library – The library, which is the control room of the house where all the information is stored, speaks of the mind. As Jesus goes into this room, He finds all kinds of trash, evil thinking, human philosophy, and other useless materials. He takes it all off the shelves, throws it away, and puts The Word of God and related materials in its place.

The Dining Room – Next He goes into the dining room, the room of the appetites and desires, and finds a worldly menu – riches, prestige, materialism, lust of the flesh, etc. He gets rid of this menu and puts the menu of God's will, which comes in many different shapes and forms. The will of God then becomes what the Christian hungers for instead of his own fleshly desires.

The Living Room – Then Jesus goes to the living room, the place of Christian fellowship and sharing, and finds that He's neglected. There's a lot of activity going on, but nobody pays any attention to Him. He's just there. The living room is where time needs to be spent with Christ. A lot of the old worldly acquaintances and wasted activities need to be cleared out, and more time spent with Christ and with people who have Christ living in them (Hebrews 10:24, 25).

The Workshop – Leaving the living room, Jesus goes to the workshop and finds fantastic tools and a beautiful workbench. However, the man is in there making only toys. So Jesus says, "You have all this ability and you can't produce anything more than a toy?" Jesus wants to take all our abilities, all our capacities, and all our capabilities, and cause them to produce things for the Kingdom – things that have eternal value. So He changes the whole format in the workshop to accomplish His work.

When He gets all done, the library is stocked with the right books, the dining room has a menu of the Will of God, the living room is settled with the fellowship of Christ and the fellowship of those who have Christ living in them, and the workshop is ready with the tools and abilities to make things for the Kingdom.

But there's a strange odor coming from somewhere. The house is nice and clean, but something stinks!!! The Lord goes over to a closet and says, "There is something dead in there." And the Christian says, "Look, you've come into my house and cleaned up everything. At least leave me one closet – that's all I ask. You can have the dining room and all those other rooms, just leave this closet alone." But the Lord says "No, I want that closet. That's the closet full of personal sins – the hidden and dead things."

The man became very angry because Jesus had every other room, but Jesus commanded him to open it. When he opened it, it was full of evil things – those little secret things that nobody knows about that go on in your mind, and that nobody sees you do. Jesus cleaned it out and when He got all done . . . then He was at home!

_____

Adapted from "My Heart, Christ's Home" by Robert Boyd Munger, 1954

Is your heart like this? Has it been cleansed and cultivated by God, and does Christ feel comfortable there? Or do you have secret places and hidden things that leave a horrible odor? When Christ asks you about these things, do you turn them over to Him for cleansing or do you lock Him out?

What does Revelation 3:20 say?_____
_____
_____
_____
_____

This verse is generally quoted as a salvation verse, but that isn't the context from which it is taken. It is a verse for believers, and pictures Christ standing outside our heart, knocking on our heart's door. Why? Because He doesn't want to barge in and clean up everything on His own. He wants our permission to enter. He wants us to welcome Him and invite Him in and to make Him feel at home.

Is Christ free to fellowship with you at any time? If so, then you truly do have a cultivated heart.

The following verses in the KJV describe what your heart will be like when it is cultivated:

G_____	Psalm 4:7
P_____	Psalm 9:1
S_____	Psalm 27:14
R_____	Psalm 28:7
C_____	Psalm 73:1
T_____	Proverbs 3:5
S_____	Proverbs 14:30
M_____	Proverbs 15:13a
P_____	Proverbs 16:1
P_____	Matthew 5:8
L_____	Matthew 22:37
H_____ and G_____	Luke 8:15
B_____	Romans 10:10
E_____	II Corinthians 4:6
T_____	Ephesians 4:32
S_____	Ephesians 5:19
T_____	Ephesians 5:20
O_____	Ephesians 6:6
P_____	Colossians 3:15
T_____	Hebrews 10:22

(answers found on page 118 if you get stuck)

A cultivated heart delights in God and has sweet fellowship with Him without hiding anything.

What does God says in Psalm 37:4?

_____

_____

What does John 5:24 tell us about what happens when our heart is cultivated and converted?

_____

_____

Our salvation depends totally upon God, knowing that we cannot save ourselves.

The following two verses should be the prayer of our hearts. Write them out and memorize them.

Psalm 51:2_____

_____

Psalm 51:10_____

_____

What does II Corinthians 5:17 tell us about God's cultivating work in our heart?_____

_____

_____

_____

Making it Personal . . .

Are there any characteristics of the cultivated heart listed on page 80 that are not consistent with your life. What can you begin to do about it?_____

_____

_____

_____

As you read through the story "Is Christ Comfortably At Home In Your Heart," which room in your heart do you need to turn over to Jesus immediately for cleansing? Are you willing to do so? Why or why not?_____

_____

_____

_____

_____

_____

_____

_____

_____

Making it Prayerful...

Dear Lord, I give you my heart. Change it, Lord. Make it beautiful and lovely - a place where I can have sweet fellowship with you. Take out all the weeds and rubble and dirt and clutter that has accumulated. Create in me a clean heart, O God, and renew a right spirit within me. I look forward to what you are going to do and Thank you for loving me enough to complete the work you've started in me.

Chapter 11

Your Hands

Hands That Are
Self Seeking

What you do with your hands tells people a lot about you. The things you grasp tightly make your values clear.

If you could only have one thing to cling to for the rest of your life, what would it be? Think of all the things that pass through your hands and choose one. For a committed Christian who wants hands of beauty, there would only be one choice - her Bible.

Some hands grab for power and riches, and shake their fist in the face of God. These are self-seeking hands. They want the best for themselves, and don't care who they push around to get it. Do you have giving hands, or grasping hands? Are you a servant or are you selfish?

We're going to take a look at two Bible characters who would be examples of hands that are self-seeking. The first one we are going to look at is a grandmother.

I think we all have expectations of what an ideal grand-mother should be doing with her hands. What are your thoughts on this?_____

_____

_____

The grandmother we are going to look at would never win the prize for "Grammie of the Year." Her name is Athaliah, and she was the daughter of the wicked Jezebel . . . remember her? Jezebel is the one that had Naboth killed because she wanted his vineyard . . . the one who stirred up her husband, King Ahab, to do evil continually. And she was the one who met her death by being thrown from a window, trampled by horses and eaten by dogs. Because Jezebel was such a bad example to her children, her daughter Athaliah turned out as bad as her mother, if not worse. She had a son named Ahaziah who became king.

Athaliah – II Chronicles 22:2 - 23:21

How does the Bible describe Athaliah as a mother?
II Chronicles 22:3; 24:7_____

_____

Athaliah's son, King Ahaziah, did evil in the sight of the Lord and only reigned one year and was killed. When he died, Athaliah decided that she wanted the throne because she sought power. What did she have to do to get what she wanted? II Chronicles 22:10

_____

_____

When you ask most women about their grandchildren, you usually have to look at pictures and listen to stories of their accomplishments. Can you imagine a woman using her hands to kill her own grandchildren!!! As she grasped for power, she became like the one she served - Satan!

What does John 8:44 tell us about Satan that shows up in Athaliah's personality?_____

_____

This is a frightening thought! If you choose not to serve God, then by default you serve Satan and there is the possibility of becoming evil like him instead of becoming holy like God.

Athaliah became queen, but how did God foil Athaliah's plans? II Chronicles 22:11-12

_____

_____

After 6 years, the King's son was brought out of hiding and made King. What was Athaliah's reaction to this?
II Chronicles 23:12-13

_____

_____

Instead of being repentant and happy to see that one of her grandchildren was still alive, she was infuriated to think that now she would lose the throne. Athaliah forgot that God is the One who sets up rulers.

Sometimes we desire a certain position or ministry for ourselves, but we need to be careful that it's God's will. When God is in control, we don't have to strive and grasp and hold on tightly. If He wants something for us, we can relax and wait for His timing.

What happened to Athaliah? II Chronicles 23:21

_____

_____

How does Galatians 6:7 apply to the way she died?

_____

_____

Athaliah will be known forever for the wickedness of her hands.

If you have a loving grandmother who is still alive, why not use your hands this week to write her a letter and tell her what she means to you and why you appreciate her.

The second Bible character we're going to look at who had self-seeking hands is:

Achan – Joshua 6 & 7

Achan's hands were greedy for money, even to the point of bringing a curse on all of Israel. When we use our hands for Satan, we not only bring shame and disgrace on ourselves, but also on our entire family. Innocent people suffer for our wrong doing.

In Joshua 6 we read the story of how the Israelites were victorious over Jericho. They had followed the Lord's instructions, and the walls of Jericho came down. Achan was among those victorious fighting men.

What other instruction from the Lord did Achan hear from the mouth of Joshua in Joshua 6:18a?

_____

_____

In Joshua 6:18b there are two reasons why Joshua warned everyone not to take of the "accursed (devoted) things." What are they?

_____

_____

_____

God's Word warns us that sin has far-reaching consequences. It not only affects us, but it affects the people around us. When we deliberately sin and go against God's Word, we no longer have God's blessing on our lives, and that puts both us and our families in danger. And secondly, it ultimately affects the whole Christian community.

For example, there were two Bible colleges that were floundering, and in both cases it was found out that leaders were involved in immorality. One college removed the leader and his family, and God once again blessed the college. The other college is liberal today and is not doing the work of God because the leader was allowed to remain without discipline.

There are churches where the pastor won't confront sin and there is no church discipline. God takes His hand of blessing from that type of church because sin isn't being dealt with. Sometimes the Pastor himself gets involved in sin, and the whole church suffers because of it. Sin has far-reaching effects.

Achan and the Israelites heard God's instructions and deliberately did not obey! What did they do, and what happened because of it? Joshua 7:1

_____

_____

_____

Joshua 7:2-5 tells the story of the Battle of Ai and how Israel was defeated because of Achan's sin. Remember, Israel had just defeated a very strong city - Jericho! Now here was this tiny town called Ai with not many people in it, and Israel was humiliated by them.

What does Joshua 7:11-12 tell us about why Israel lost this battle?_____

_____

_____

_____

_____

Read back through Joshua 7:2-5 to discover who suffered unnecessarily because of Achan's sin.

_____

Not only did these 36 men suffer, but also their families and friends. That would be a possible 36 husbands who never went home to their wives. 36 fathers who would never see their children again. Maybe 36 sets (72) of parents who would mourn the loss of their sons. Friends and other relatives who would be saddened and feel a sense of loss.

Because of one man's sin, all this sorrow came. And with that sorrow, came loss of confidence to all of Israel! As usual, when Satan tempts us with sin, he does not let us know the consequences!

When Joshua heard about Israel's defeat, he had each family come one by one in order to question them. What was Achan's confession when questioned? Joshua 7:20-21

_____

_____

_____

_____

_____

Achan had sinfully taken beautiful garments, silver and gold and buried them because he wanted them and allowed himself to imagine himself with them. He couldn't even enjoy them because they were "accursed." Maybe he thought he could dig them up later and be able to enjoy them when the people, and God, had forgotten about it. Sometimes we try to hide sin or ignore it, thinking that God will eventually let us off the hook.

The four steps of Achan's sin:	
He Saw	He let his eyes linger on and admire something God said he couldn't have
He Coveted	He wanted it for himself
He Took	He deliberately sinned (actions follow thoughts)
He Hid	He tried to cover up his sin

> *"Be not deceived, God is not mocked*
> *Whatever you sow, you shall reap!"*
> Galatians 6:7

Because of Achan's great sin before the Lord, what happened to him and all his family? Joshua 7:24-26

_____

_____

_____

What do you think really destroyed Achan?

_____

_____

Matthew 6:19-20 gives us some good advice:

> *"Do not store up for yourselves treasures on earth, where moth and rust destroy, and where thieves break in and steal. But store up for yourselves treasures in heaven..."*

Achan did not rely on God to supply all his needs - he wanted more and took things into his own hands. When we do that, we show the root of ugliness that is in our hearts.

After the problem of Achan was dealt with, God turned from His anger, and in chapter 8, we read that Joshua and the children of Israel defeated the town of Ai because God was on their side.

One final sobering thought found in Mark 9:43. Write out this verse:

_____

_____

_____

_____

_____

In other words, recognize and deal with your sin while there is time in whatever way you have to! As a new Christian, I remember praying to God "Lord I pray that you will do whatever it takes to get rid of this sin from my life, even if it means bringing me home to heaven." Somehow I knew instinctively that it was better to let God deal with my sin strongly than allow it to continue to hurt myself and others.

Making it personal . . .
If God were to write a chapter about you in the Bible about how you use your hands, what positive and negative things would he write?

Is there something you need to confess to God as sin and ask Him to help you overcome? Do it now while there is still time. Are you willing to allow Him to deal with it in any way He deems necessary?

Making it prayerful . . .

Dear Lord, help me to dedicate my hands to serving you and not grasping for my own selfish desires. Thank you for your wonderful grace, mercy, forgiveness, and restoration that makes it possible for me to be cleansed and to start afresh each day. Help me to have hands that will serve others and glorify you.

Chapter 12

Your Hands
Hands That Serve Others

Beautiful hands serve God by loving and serving others. This is quite a contrast to the wicked hands we have already studied.

Name some ways we can serve others with our hands:

In this chapter we're going to take a look at two women who are an example of how to use our hands in serving.

The Virtuous Woman – Proverbs 31:10-31

The Virtuous Woman had three beauty secrets:
- *She feared the Lord*
- *She loved her family and took good care of them*
- *She worked hard with her hands to meet needs of those around her*

All three beauty secrets are important to a woman who wants lasting beauty.

In Proverbs 31, it refers to hands in 12 verses! If God put this much emphasis on hands, He considers it very important.

Look at the following verses and write down how the Virtuous Woman uses her hands:

v. 13 _____

No-one has to force her to work, and she doesn't complain about it. She volunteers cheerfully to do what needs to be done.

v. 14 _____

She's not out buying junk food from fast food places, but looks for nutritious, interesting, and colorful food of different textures that would appeal to her family and be good for them.

v. 15 _____

She isn't lazy. She sets the pace for her household instead of lying around waiting for people to wait on her. She faces the day cheerfully and positively. The world says "Be a princess!" God says "Be a servant!"

v. 16 _____

She takes a barren field and makes something useful and fruitful out of it. She is creative.

v. 17 _____

She is not the fragile type that thinks women should be waited on. She is a strong, healthy woman who exercises and is full of vitality. She takes her health seriously.

v. 19 _____

She is creative and diligent. She does what is necessary to provide for her family.

v. 20 _____

She watches out for people she can help. She takes the initiative to seek them out and doesn't wait for someone to ask her for help. She's not only concerned for her own family "Us four and no more", but she looks at people with the compassionate eyes of Christ.

v. 21 _____

She wants her family to be warm in the winter and looks ahead to their comfort. Because of her creativity and skill, they can wear better clothing than what she could afford if she bought all their clothing ready-made.

v. 22 _____

She honors her husband by looking as nice as she can without overspending. (She knows that man looks on the outward appearance - I Samuel 16:7b)

v. 24 _____

She is a business woman and makes extra money by working out of her home. She knows what she is good at and uses her talents and gifts effectively in all areas of her life.

v. 27 _____

She doesn't sit around watching the "soaps" and over-eating. She isn't bored or complaining or on the phone gossiping. She is a fulfilled and happy woman because "Whatever her hand finds to do, she does it with all her might (Eccles. 9:10)." She is enthusiastic about life.

v. 31 _____

Because of the good things she does with her hands, she will not only be praised now, but also later when she stands before the Lord. She will hear the words, "Well done, good and faithful servant."

We can learn from the Virtuous Woman not to sit around, bored with life, wondering where we can find some excitement. God wants us to be hard working, diligent women, always ready to serve others with our hands.

What does Hebrews 6:10 tell us?_____

_____

_____

_____

_____

The next time you are bored and looking for something to do, find something to do with your hands and do it with all your might. You will find great satisfaction, joy and excitement in keeping busy and working for the Lord. You will be a happier person, and those around you will be impressed.

Now, look back over your list of what the Virtuous Woman does with her hands, and determine the area or areas that you need to improve in, or maybe even learn for the first time. Write these down and purpose in your heart to become more like the Virtuous Woman this year.

- It could be in the area of attitude. Being able to work willingly instead of complaining. Purpose that you will refuse to complain when someone asks you to do something, and that you will cheerfully do it.

- Maybe you need to plan out your meals for a day or for a week at a time so that you and your family eat healthy. Look up recipes, write out your meal plan, clip coupons, and go shopping. Then follow through and make some deliciousness.

- Purpose to get up earlier than the rest of your family for the purpose of spending time with God and planning your day. Then surprise everyone by having breakfast ready, with some soft music in the background, and a cheerful smile on your face.

- Maybe you've never had the joy of planting things and watching them grow. You could try to beautify a corner of your yard with flowers, or choose a small plot and plant some veggies.

- Bone up on nutrition and exercise and put what you learn into practice. Sit less...move more.

- Perhaps you need help in the area of sewing. If you haven't sewed before, plan and learn how to make something simple. If you already know how to sew, purpose to make most of your gifts this year.

- Look around you and see who has needs, and then try to meet those needs. Help a widow or someone needy in your community and make doing good works a continuous practice in your life.

- If you have a problem with being bored and not satisfied with your life, start listing everything that needs to be done or projects that you would like to do – cleaning, organizing, decorating. As you go to your list and start accomplishing the things on it, you'll be come a much more interesting and accomplished person.

A virtuous woman first uses her hands to open her Bible, then to provide for people's needs.

In doing this she fulfills what two commandments? Matthew 22:37-40

_____

_____

_____

Another woman in the Bible who delighted in good works by using her hands was:

Dorcas – Acts 9:36-42

We find out more about Dorcas by the meaning of her name. It means "gazelle." A gazelle is a small antelope, swift and graceful, with large lustrous eyes.

Dorcas might have been tiny and feminine, but she was also mighty. She looked at people with compassion and recognized their needs. She did things quickly and well and had no time for idleness.

Her beauty secrets:

- *She feared the Lord*
- *She worked hard with her hands to meet the needs of those around her*

How she used her hands:
v. 36 _____

Good works – things done for other people who have needs
Almsdeeds – deeds of mercy to the poor, involving money, food, clothes, or other needs the poor might have

v. 39 _____

Dorcas used her hands to help widows - women both young and old who were struggling to survive without their husbands. They had lost someone they loved, and Dorcas was their friend who came alongside of them during difficult times and tried to help them and meet their needs.

What happens in Acts 9:37?

_____

What scene did Peter come upon in Acts 9:39?

_____

_____

_____

These widows really appreciated what Dorcas did with her hands and wondered what they would do without her.

God appreciated her ministry as well. What does Acts 9:40-42 tell us?

_____

_____

What does James 1:27 tell us about what God considers pure and true religion to be?

_____

_____

_____

_____

Not only had these widows lost their husbands, but some of them probably had children to raise alone. What a lonely time that is for a woman, and a friend like Dorcas would be a great blessing.

Making it personal . . .

In Exodus 4:2, the Lord asks Moses, "What is that in thine hand?" He is asking that same question of you today.

"Woman, what is that in thine hand?"

Is it a sewing machine, a textbook, a songbook, a paintbrush, a pen, a steering wheel, a dustcloth, a mixing bowl, a laptop, a diaper, an iron . . . your Bible? Whatever it is, God wants you to use it for His glory.

Determine what is in your hand (what things you do best), and write down ways you can serve God and others.

_____

_____

_____

_____

_____

_____

_____

_____

_____

Making it Prayerful . . .

Dear Lord, I give you my hands to be used for your honor and glory. With your help, I will keep so busy loving and serving others, that I will never lack for things to do. Help me to see the needs of others and to help out whenever I can. And I pray that when people see my good works, that You will get the glory.

Chapter 13

Your Mind
The Control Center of Your Body - Part 1

*"And be ye transformed by the renewing
of your mind, that ye may prove what is
that good and acceptable, and perfect
will of God."*
Romans 12:2

Whatever you fill your mind with is going to eventually show up in all the other parts of your body. "Garbage in, garbage out" can refer to your mind.

If you're dishonest in your mind, eventually your hands will steal or your lips will lie. If you're rebellious in your mind, your feet will eventually take you to the wrong places, you'll be saying things you shouldn't say, you'll be listening to things you shouldn't be listening to. All the different parts of your body will be doing things that are not pleasing to God.

In Philippians 4:8 (KJV), God gives us specific instructions as to what we are to think about:

> "Finally brethren,
> Whatever things are _____
> Whatever things are _____
> Whatever things are _____
> Whatever things are _____
> Whatever things are _____
> Whatever things are of _____ _____
> If there be any _____
> And if there be any _____
> Think on these things!

During this study, we have been looking at Biblical examples of people who have used different parts of their bodies in opposition to God. The reason for each person's failure was ultimately because they fed their minds with the garbage of the world and the enemy's lies, instead of what is taught in Philippians 4:8.

Our first lesson was on eyes. See if you can write down what each of the following people focused on with their eyes and thought about in their minds before they sinned:

Eve -

Potiphar's wife -

Lot's wife -

King David -

Then we studied about ears. We looked at the unbelievers in Noah's day and how their minds were evil continuously. They listened to the voice of Satan instead of the voice of God. Unbelievers today do the same thing. They fill their minds with things that are not good.

All the other parts of the body we studied were the same way. Each person who sinned needed to have their mind renewed so that the other parts of their body would not sin.

In this chapter we're going to focus on how we can renew our minds so that our total person can be transformed to glorify God. Transformation begins and ends with God's Word. It is the power behind any change in our lives.

You're probably saying to yourself "Here we go again - have a quiet-time, memorize Scripture, study God's Word!"

And you're right . . . here we go again! It always gets back to that. There are no shortcuts to becoming a truly beautiful woman of God.

Solomon who was the wisest man in the world, concluded the Book of Ecclesiastes with these verses in Eccl.12:13-14

"Let us hear the conclusion of the whole matter:
Fear God and keep His commandments;
for this is the whole duty of man.
For God shall bring every work into judgment,
with every secret thing,
whether it be good or whether it be evil."

Think about this for a moment. Solomon probably had more sex than anyone else - he had 700 wives and concubines. He had great wisdom and fame in ruling God's people - Kings and queens from all the earth came to him and bowed down before his wisdom. He could buy anything he wanted - the best furniture, the best food, the best clothes; anything he wanted he could have. He could travel anywhere without worrying about money. Everyone respected him.

And yet, what did he say the whole conclusion of life is?

_____

_____

What did he say would happen at the Judgment?

_____

_____

_____

When we stand before God and the things of earth have passed away, fearing God and keeping His commandments is all that will matter. Our entire life is going to be reduced to these two things, and we will be rewarded or lose rewards accordingly at the Judgment.

So let us once again think about the Word of God - what it is, what it does, and what we need to do with it.

God's Word is inspired - II Timothy 3:16; II Peter 1:21

God superintended the writing of Scripture so that it would be without error.

Not only the ideas, but the very words of Scripture are inspired. No word is used by accident or just by chance. The Bible is the exact record of the mind and will of God.

God's Word is revealed -Deuteronomy 29:29

The Bible is God revealing Himself to man and telling man truth which he could not otherwise know.

We can know there is a God by looking at creation, but we need the Bible to tell us about Jesus, about sin, about what God expects from us.

God's Word is illumined - I Corinthians 2:11b,12

When you receive Christ as your personal Savior, you receive the presence and ministry of the Holy Spirit in your life, enabling you to understand the Word of God.

God's Word does many supernatural and miraculous things. No other book can do what God's Word can do in our lives.

It cleanses and purifies

Ephesians 5:26 speaks of "the water of the Word." It cleans out your mind and replaces evil thoughts with God's thoughts.

As a new Christian I graduated from Word of Life Bible Institute in upstate NY. Most of my time there was spent in the Word studying and memorizing it. By the time I graduated, God had taken away my worldly and unrighteous thoughts and replaced them with His cleansing Word. My mind was renewed.

It illuminates and guides

Psalm 119:105 speaks of the Bible as the light and the lamp.

If you want to discover God's will for your life, get into God's Word - it will guide you on a daily basis. Through His Word, God will direct you in the way you should go, and will not leave you to stumble around in darkness.

It nourishes, satisifies and sustains

I Peter 2:2, John 6:35 and Hebrews 5:12-14 speak of the milk, bread and meat of the Word.

Just as you need good nutrition to sustain your physical health, you need to have a balanced diet of God's Word to have good spiritual health. Just think of your improved spiritual health if you ate three balanced meals of the Word of God each day!

It reveals

James 1:23-25 speaks of the Bible as a mirror.

It reveals all our imperfections, for we see ourselves as we really are - sinners in need of a Savior, and sheep in need of a Shepherd.

It equips for warfare

Hebrews 4:12 speaks of the Bible as a sword and Ephesians 6:10-18 tells us that we need to put on the whole armor of God in order to defeat the enemy.

We are in a battle, and Satan is our enemy who is continually trying to trip us up and make us ineffective for God.

It equips us for work

Jeremiah 23:29b speaks of the Bible as a hammer.

You have work to do in the service of the Lord, and the Bible will equip you to do that work, whether it is building up other believers or evangelizing the lost. The only lasting work you will do here on earth is in the power of the Holy Spirit directed by the Word of God.

It reproduces

I Peter 1:23 speaks of the Bible as seed.

God's Word is able to produce new children into God's family. That's what it means to be "born again." When we accept Christ as Savior, we are born as new children into the family of God. No person is ever "born again" apart from God's Word.

We've seen what God's Word is and what it can do for us. Now we need to think about our responsibility to God's Word.

Look up the following verses and see if you can figure out

the one word answers that tell us our responsibility. You might even find the answer in the description following it.

Psalm 85:8 - H_____

We need to take every opportunity to hear the Word of God. This includes church, life group/Sunday school, Bible studies and conferences.

Isaiah 34:16 - R_____

A good goal would be to read through the Bible once a year. This gives you an overall view and ties together the Old and New Testaments.

II Timothy 2:15 - S_____

Work hard at digging out the treasures of wisdom from God's Word. It is better than gold or silver or rubies or anything else we may desire (Proverbs 3:13-18). It is valuable.

Psalm 119:11 - M_____

Hide God's Word in your heart so that it can never be taken away from you, and the Holy Spirit will be able to bring it to your mind at the moment you need it.

Psalm 1:2 - M_____

Think about what you have learned in the Word of God throughout the day. Talk to God about it. Ponder it's meaning and how it applies to your life.

Jeremiah 26:13a - O_____

Very simply, do what God tells you to do. Don't be a rebellious child. God says this proves your love for Him.

Psalm 119:97 - L_____

Hold God's Word in high esteem. Let it be the one thing you cling to and are devoted to.

John 12:36 - B_____

Trust God's Word is true because of God's character. God is good all the time!

Psalm 119:16 - D_____ in
Get excited and passionate about God's Word. Look forward to spending time with God.

Now go back and put a star next to any of the responsibilities you need to improve on and ask God for His help.

<u>Reasons to study and obey God's Word</u>
(Look up and write out the verses)

To know God's will - Psalm 32:8

_____
_____
_____

To receive desires of our heart - Psalm 37:4

_____
_____
_____

To show our love for God - John 14:15_____

_____

To show we've spent time with Jesus - Acts 4:13

_____
_____
_____
_____
_____

To increase in faith - Romans 10:17

_____
_____

God commands us to - II Timothy 2:15

_____

_____

_____

_____

To overcome philosophies of the world - I John 5:4

_____

_____

_____

Who Should Read The Bible?

The Young - to learn how to live
The Old - to know how to die
The Ignorant - for wisdom
The Learned - for humility
The Rich - for compassion
The Poor - for comfort
The Dreamer - for enchantment
The Practical - for counsel
The Weak - for strength
The Strong - for direction
The Haughty - for warning
The Humble - for exaltation
The Troubled - for peace
The Weary - for rest
The Sinner - for salvation
The Doubting - for assurance
All Christians - for guidance

Chapter 14

Your Mind
The Control Center of Your Body - Part 2

*"And be ye transformed by the renewing
of your mind, that ye may prove what is
that good and acceptable, and perfect
will of God."*
Romans 12:2

HOW TO STUDY GOD'S WORD

Study the Bible through - Never begin a day
Without mastering a verse from its pages.

Pray it in - Never lay aside your Bible until the verse
or passage you have studied has become a part of you.

Work it out - Live the truth you get in the morning
throughout each hour of the day.

Pass it on - Seek to tell somebody else what you have
learned.

MAKE THIS TIME WITH GOD A . . .

Practical time - choose a time that is convenient for you,
not when you know you will be interrupted.

Priority time - Stick with it! Treat it as an important
appointment with God, and keep that appointment
no matter what!

Peaceful and Private time - Choose a quiet place and make
it a time of total concentration on God and what He is
going to reveal to you.

Persistent time – Ask God to teach you as you study
a passage of Scripture, and purpose not to
get up until He does.

Personal time – Make Psalm 119:18 the daily prayer of
your time with God. "Open my eyes, Lord, that I
may see wondrous things in your Law"

PRIMARY TOOL:

An attitude of excitement and enthusiasm as
you seek wisdom from God

Get excited! The God of the universe wants to
communicate with you. He will have a special
message for you and show you wonderful things.

The Bible is the only book whose author is always
present when you read it.

OTHER TOOLS:

Pens, pencils, eraser, notebook, dictionary, ruler,
concordance, highlighter, topical Bible, atlas,
and the Bible you will study from.

A FEW BIBLE STUDY METHODS:

1. Proverbs Study – Under headings such as Wise, Foolish, Angry, Slothful, Virtuous, Righteous, etc., write out verses from Proverbs that pertain to them. You will gain valuable insight into your character, and the character of those around you.

2. Psalms Study – Select a Psalm and read it through 2 or 3 times. Answer the following questions:
   Is there an example for me to follow?
   Is there a commandment for me to obey?
   Is there a sin for me to forsake?
   Is there a promise for me to claim?

3. Biographical Study - Choose a person in the Bible to study. For example, you might want to learn more about Rebekah, Rahab, Dorcas, or the Queen of Sheba.

   Read every Scripture passage there is regarding her.
   Write down her faults and her good qualities.
   What was her attitude towards God and those in authority over her?
   What contribution did she make to those around her?
   In what ways was she a good example or bad example?
   How will she always be remembered?
   What does this person teach me about myself?

4. Topical Study - Choose a topic and follow it throughout the Bible. Write down your insights. Develop an outline. Naves Topical Bible is a good resource for this type of study.

5. Book Study - Choose a book of the Bible to study. Do chapter titles, theme, outline, word studies, etc.

BASICS OF INDUCTIVE BIBLE STUDY

Inductive Bible study involves three skills:
Observation - Discover what it says
Interpretation - Discover what it means
Application - Discover how it works

A. **Observation** - Discover what it says

Step 1: Begin With Prayer - Always ask God to teach you as you open the Scriptures.

Step 2: Ask the "5 W's and an H"
Who is speaking? Who is this about? Who are the main characters? And to whom are they speaking?

What is the subject or event covered in the chapter. What do you learn about the people, the event, or the teaching from the text? What instructions are given?

When do or will the events occur? When did or will something happen to a particular person, people or nation?

Where did or will this happen? Where was it said?

Why is something being said or mentioned? Why will this happen? Why at this time? Why this person or nation?

How will it happen? How is it to be done? How is it illustrated?

Step 3: Mark Key Words and Phrases - A key word or phrase is one that is essential to the text, and when removed, leaves the passage empty of meaning.

Step 4: Look for Lists - the best way to discover lists in the text is to observe how a key word is described, note what is said about someone or something, or group related thoughts or instructions.

Step 5: Watch for Contrasts and Comparisons - A contrast is looking at things that are different or opposite such as light/darkness or wise/foolish. The word "but" often signifies that a contrast is being made.

A comparison points out similarities and is often indicated by the use of words such as "like" or "as."

Step 6: Note Expressions of Time - The timing of something can be observed by exact statements about the time, or by words such as *until, then, when* and *after.*

Step 7: Identify Terms of Conclusion - these usually

114

follow an important sequence of thought and include words such as *wherefore, therefore, for this reason,* and *finally.* You should be able to look through the preceding verses and summarize the message.

Step 8: Develop Chapter Themes - Try to express the theme as briefly as possible, using words found in the text.

Step 9: Discover Life Lessons - The Holy Spirit will bring to your attention truths that God wants you to be aware of and live by in your own life.

Step 10: Complete an "At A Glance" Chart - This provides a compact visual summary of the book that you can return to again and again for easy reference.

~ Record the author of the book
~ Record the date the book was written
~ Record the key words
~ Record the chapter themes
~ Record the purpose of the book
~ Record the main theme of the book

B. **Interpretation** - Discover what it means

1 - Remember the context rules - Be prepared to consider each verse in the light of the surrounding verses, the book in which it is found, the entire Word of God.

2 - Always seek the full counsel of the Word of God - As you become more familiar with the whole counsel of God's Word, you will be able to discern whether a teaching is Biblical or not.

3 - Remember that Scripture will never contradict Scripture.
4 - Don't base your convictions on an obscure passage of Scripture.
5 - Interpret Scripture literally - the Bible is not a book of

mysticism. Take the Word of God at face value in its natural, normal sense.

6 - Look for the single meaning of the passage - Let the passage speak for itself and look for the meaning.

C. APPLICATION - Discover how it works

1 - What does the passage teach?

2 - Does this section of Scripture expose any error in my beliefs or in my behavior?

3 - What is God's instruction to me as His child?

4 - When applying Scripture, beware of the following:

~ Applying cultural standards rather than Biblical standards
~ Attempting to strengthen a legitimate truth by using a Scripture incorrectly
~ Applying Scripture out of prejudice from past training or teaching

---

Once you get a taste of what God can do in your life through Bible study and prayer, you'll never be satisfied with a mediocre Christian life again.

Making it Personal. . .

God wants us to present our bodies a living sacrifice to Him and let Him transform each part into a member fit for His use. The key is willingness and obedience to what God tells us to do.

Is there something in your life that you need to turn over to God so He can make you more beautiful? Are you straddling the fence in your walk with Him with one foot in the world? Honestly examine your own heart and confess any known sin, asking for God's forgiveness and direction.

As we willingly submit to His direction in our lives, we will find ourselves being transformed into beautiful butterflies, being set free from our cocoon of sin.

Making it Prayerful. . .

Father, I thank you for your Word and its transforming power in my life. Help me to be enthusiastic about studying, memorizing, and especially obeying it. Help me to delight myself in you, always eager to hear what you have to say to me, knowing that you love me and want my life to be of value. Help me to remember what I have learned from this study, especially the fact that Satan never tells me the truth. Help me to trust more in You. Amen.

Answer Page

Page 19, 20
Sovereign, Righteous, Just, Love, Eternal, Omniscient, Omnipresent, Omnipotent, Immutable, Truth

Page 39
Joy, peace, comfort, laughing, glory, honor, gladness, strength, salvation, wisdom, song, hope, love, Holy Spirit, good name, long life, riches, crown

Page 64
Being slow to speak shows we have: wisdom, humility, love

Page 83
Glad
Praising
Strong
Rejoicing
Clean
Trusting
Sound
Merry
Prepared
Pure
Loving
Honest and good
Believing
Enlightened
Tender
Singing
Thankful
Obedient
Peaceful
True

www.ingramcontent.com/pod-product-compliance
Lightning Source LLC
Chambersburg PA
CBHW051838040426
42447CB00006B/598